VELVET

BY TOM RATCLIFFE

Published by Playdead Press 2019

© Tom Ratcliffe 2019

Tom Ratcliffe has asserted his rights under the
Copyright, Design and Patents Act, 1988, to be
identified as the author of this work.

A CIP catalogue record for this book is available from
the British Library.

ISBN 978-1-910067-73-4

Playdead Press
www.playdeadpress.com

VELVET

by Tom Ratcliffe

CAST:

TOM   Tom Ratcliffe

CREATIVE:

DIRECTOR   Andrew Twyman
PRODUCERS   Tom Ratcliffe &
                                       Jenna Fincken for work.Theatre
DESIGNER   Luke W Robson
LIGHTING DESIGNER   Jack Weir
SOUND DESIGNER   Callum Wyles
STAGE MANAGER   Gemma Scott (Pleasance Courtyard)
                                       Juliet Heap (VAULT Festival)

VELVET was first performed at the Pleasance Courtyard as part of Edinburgh Festival Fringe 2018 in a production by work.Theatre.

work.Theatre would like to thank the following for their help on the production: *Harlow Playhouse, HighTide, English Touring Theatre, Robert & Vina Myson and Genie & Richard Hunte.*

Tom Ratcliffe | Writer & TOM

Writing credits include: *VELVET* (Pleasance Courtyard), *Gifted* (Pleasance Theatre) & *Circa* (Theater de Meervaart, Amsterdam and The Vaults Theatre). Tom was shortlisted for the Old Vic 12 in 2016 and longlisted for the Verity Bargate & Papatango awards in 2017. Short plays have included runs at Theatre503, Old Red Lion Theatre & St James Theatre.

Acting credits include: *VELVET* (Pleasance Courtyard), *Sket* (Park Theatre), *5 Guys Chillin'* (Kings Head Theatre / Assembley Roxy) and *Wars of the Roses* (Rose Theatre Kingston). Film credits include *Once Upon a Time in London* (Gateway Films).

Andrew Twyman | Director

VELVET (Pleasance Courtyard), *Deserts* (HighTide/ Latitude Festival), *Kanye the First* (HighTide), *Odd Shaped Balls* (Old Red Lion), *Don't Smoke in Bed* (Finborough Theatre), *Te Karakia* (Finborough Theatre – part of Vibrant Festival).

Credits as associate include: *Sugar Coated Bullets of the Bourgeoisie* (HighTide / Arcola Theatre).

Jenna Fincken | Co-Producer

Jenna has been part of the work.Theatre team since our inaugural showing of *Circa* at the Theater de Meervaart in 2016. Jenna has co-produced *Gifted* (Pleasance Theatre) and *VELVET* (Pleasance Courtyard) in that time. Jenna trained and works as an actor, graduating from The Oxford School of Drama in 2015.

Luke W Robson | Designer

Luke's credits a designer include: *Electrolyte* (UK Tour), *VELVET* (Pleasance Courtyard / VAULT Festival & UK Tour), *It's True, It's True, It's True* (New Diorama / Underbelly), *Madame Butterfly* (Kings Head Theatre), *Unspoken* (Theatre Royal Newcastle), *The Terminal Velocity of Snowflakes* (Live Theatre).

Jack Weir | Lighting Designer

The Funeral Director (Papatango), *Dust* (Trafalgar Studios / Soho Theatre), *The Plague* (Arcola Theatre), *Rain Man* (Theatre Royal Windsor & UK Tour), *Rothschild and Sons* (Park Theatre), *Hanna* (Arcola Theatre), *Georges Marvellous Medicine* (Leicester Curve & Tour), *Talk Radio* (Old Red Lion), *Summer in London* (Theatre Royal Stratford East), *Judy* (Arts Theatre West End), *Assata Taught Me* (Gate Theatre), *The Boys in the Band* (Vaudeville Theatre).

Callum Wyles | Sound Designer

VELVET (Pleasance Courtyard), *No one is Coming to Save You* (This Noise), *The Immigrant* (Chris Michael), *Romeo and Juliet* (South Hill Park), *Boom* (Theatre503), *Beauty and the Beast* (South Hill Park).

work.Theatre

work.Theatre are an internationally produced theatre company specialising in new writing. work.Theatre's first full-length production *Circa* premièred at the Theater de Meervaart, Amsterdam in January 2016 as part of Festival Contact. *Circa* then transferred to The Vaults Theatre in June 2016. Our second production, Gifted premiered at The Pleasance, Islington as part of their inaugural season of the 'Downstairs' Theatre in May 2018. Later the same year Tom Ratcliffe's *VELVET* ran at The Pleasance Courtyard as part of the Edinburgh Fringe Festival. The run was highly successful, resulting in multiple 5 star reviews and the play winning the 'Outstanding Monologue' accolade in Theatre Weekly's 'Best of the Fest'.

For my wonderful family, Ben and Jenna.
Thank you for always believing in me.

CHARACTERS

Tom

NOTES ON TEXT

Tom is the character speaking unless specified otherwise. Other characters can be recorded voices or played by Tom.

Pauses and beats are indicated by the space given between lines.

I'm a superstar because I'm super at being a star

I'm a superstar because I'm super at being a star

I'm a superstar because I'm super at being a star

I'm a-
How many times do you want me to do this?

VOICE: Once more
Can we have more emphasis on the words beginning
with S?

Super and star?

VOICE: And superstar

Right

I'm a superstar because I'm super at being a star

VOICE: Super
Okay so now you're a rising star. You're fresh, you're
new, you're hot
The actor equivalent of Kanye or Justin Bieber
You like to get a little bit down and dirty
You've just won 'Artist of the Year' Punked awards
And no it's not the TV show. It's a new clothing
brand
So I want you to take this wind-up torch
That's your prop. That's the award
And I want you to go outside
Come back in

Lots of energy
And give the thank you speech of your life

MAN: I've seen you before

Have you?

MAN: Yeah

Okay
Do you mean on here or
I think you might be mistaking me for someone else.
I don't really
This isn't usually my thing

MAN: I'm not
It was definitely you

Is this another
You're gonna say I look like someone

MAN: No

People say I look like Tom Daly without the body

MAN: I've seen you
In real life
You're hot

Thanks
Where?

MAN: Around

Like?

MAN: On the street
I've seen you around
I'm glad we're talking

Press night
My first one
And I'm obviously determined to be belle of the ball
I'm wearing a fucking great shirt and I know I look
fit
I look in the mirror and I know that if I was a man
who wasn't so naturally passive
I would want to fuck me
I kind of do anyway

Well maybe want me to fuck me

The play I'm doing is so much fun
I've been cast as the leader of a London suburb gang
who gets girls to send him naked videos before
exposing them on the internet
I even force kids to sell drugs
Typecasting these days
But asides from being put in an obvious box
It's a male lead at a great theatre and I still don't
have an agent

11

And tonight this room is full of them
So it's really fucking important

Marcus

My best friend from drama school who did really well
out of showcase
Meetings with literally everyone
The annoying thing is he's actually really good
One of those people that doesn't have to put the work
in but somehow gets it right and everyone loves him
anyway
Was supposed to come tonight and bring his agent
But he cancelled last minute
His agent's taking him to an industry party instead
so

Tonight was even more important because I have a
casting director who really liked me at drama school
in and I was kind of looking forward to the moral
support
Even more disastrously Marcus cancelled so last
minute that I couldn't find anyone decent to take the
ticket
So I had to give it to mum instead
She couldn't find anyone to look after the dog either
So she arrived genuinely expecting to bring the beast
into the theatre
And when the beast
More affectionately known as Lexi
Was turned away
I found mum bargaining with a homeless man outside
to dog-sit

She offered him fifty quid
Twenty up front and thirty plus a bottle of absolut
vodka upon collection

He's not here
I can't
Two tickets he definitely had
Box office said they were both picked up

MUM: Here's my handsome star

She's not what you would expect my mum to sound
like

MUM: I won't say anything whilst you do your
Developmental chats

Networking

MUM: Networking chats
I can just stand here in silence so you're not on your
own
How does that sound?

Fine
That sounds fine mum

MUM: I thought the girl playing your opposite number
Pretty
Curly dark hair
Was really excellent

She always does this

13

She lists off what she thought of everyone else except
me until I ask for her opinion
This stems from when she described my turn as the
purple plum in our year five showing of the hungry
caterpillar as unrooted
I usually don't entertain it but tonight I need her to
validate me

And?

MUM: And what?

What did you think?

MUM: Of?

Me

MUM: You looked so handsome

Bitch

MUM: I wasn't a fan of whatever accent you were trying to
do

Bitch

MUM: Yes it kind of distracted from anything else you were
doing
Not like the other girl who just was
Sounded like a bad Jamaican

Fucking bitch

MUM: But I couldn't be prouder of my handsome boy

MUM: Do I embarrass you?

No mum

MUM: I do. I'm an embarrassment to you

You're not. Don't be silly
It's just

You're a bitch

I don't like these things
And it looks like he's gone anyway
So

MUM: I'll get you a beer
We can have a toast in the corner and I'll take you home
And if I come back and I see you talking to anyone
I'll go and spend time with Lexi and Francis. How does that sound?

Who's Francis?

MUM: The nice man looking after Lexi
Stop being a silly sod and go and talk to people

Fuck
Come on Tom you bellend

DAMIEN: Tom
  I thought you'd gone

  Damien
  Thank you so much for coming

  At last
  My moment

DAMIEN: Our pleasure
    Thank you for the tickets
    You were excellent

    Thank you
    That's very kind of you

DAMIEN: Tom this is Rebecca

REBECCA: It's incredible just how different you are in person

DAMIEN: Yes Tom I wasn't expecting such a transformation
    I'm very impressed
    Any agent interest?

    This is where I fell down last time
    When I first met him I didn't have any
    I told him that I had no interest and then I was never
    seen for anything

I've got a couple coming
A few sniffs here and there

Sniffs?

DAMIEN: Well you've got one here

Jackpot

Did you
Um
Did you enjoy the show?

REBECCA: I did Tom
You were very good indeed
You're exciting because I could put you up for a lot
of things
Damien has told me in no uncertain terms that if I
sign you he would call you into a lot of rooms

Great

REBECCA: Obviously we need to have a meeting first
I have to run now but how is Monday for you?

Monday's brill

Brill
Who the fuck says brill

REBECCA: Great
Nine o'clock
I'll see you then

    Great
    I'll
    See you then

    Thank you so much
    This is really
    This is so kind of you

DAMIEN: No problem at all
    I'm happy to help
    And you proved me right tonight. That was excellent
    work

DAMIEN: Are you with your friends?

    Sorry?

DAMIEN: Tonight
    Are you with your friends?

    No. No
    Just me

DAMIEN: Aren't they laying on a big party?

    This is it
    The bar stops serving at eleven

DAMIEN: Right
    So we don't have time for one more?

    I can try and get us-

DAMIEN: Well look
    I live around the corner

If you excuse the mess you could always come back
to mine
We can have a drink there

DAMIEN: It would be great to get to know you a bit better
The man behind the mask

DAMIEN: It's up to you
Do you want to?

Yeah
Um
Yes

DAMIEN: Great

I just need to check what time I'm working in the
morning
Fringe theatre

DAMIEN: You don't have to

No. No
I just

I start at eight

DAMIEN: That's okay

We'll have to meet for coffee or something

DAMIEN: If you want to

You don't look American
You look sort of
Not German but something Germanic
Maybe Austrian
Probably Hungarian?

MAN: I look Hungarian?

I'd believe you were Canadian

MAN: Lol I'm not Canadian

When an American's attractive they usually have a
well-built face in a sort of wide square Ryan Gosling
way
You're narrow and angular

MAN: Thanks?

It's a good thing

MAN: So you think I'm hot?

Objectively yes
In a purely observational sense

MAN: So you're here to observe?

I'm not here for
I'm not looking for anything

MAN: Then why do you keep talking to me?

        You have a narrow angular face

MAN: I haven't seen you in the street

        Sorry?

MAN: I read your bio
        I haven't seen you on the street
        I've seen the show

        Are you fan girling?

MAN: Are you an advertising profile?
        I thought you were the actor pictured

        That is me
        But yes
        Advertising
        They made us download it
        Even the straight guys
        Quite funny really
        It's a gay play so obviously the way to pull in an
        audience is to advertise it as potential sex on grindr

MAN: You're really talented
        I was going to stick around and say hi but my
        colleague was with me
        I would have wanted you to myself

Did you like the show?

MAN: I did
I got hard as I watched you

MAN: Are you just here for advertising?

Yes

MAN: Shame
You're very talented

You said

MAN: I'm currently scouting

Scouting?

MAN: Yes
For my job
I'm scouting

For what?

MAN: Talent
Acting talent

What did you say your name was again?

MAN: Who says I told you my name?

MAN: Can we move to whatsapp?

Matthew and I have been together for three years
And by that I mean mostly
About a year and half in Matthew decided I wasn't
meeting his emotional needs for around six months
before he finally realised he was punching above his
weight regardless and came crawling back
And by crawling back I mean he took me back after I
wouldn't stop crying outside his work for two hours
He's an investment banker and considering the vast
majority of his colleagues are both straight and
emotionally stunted
That would have been really embarrassing for him

Matthew's biggest strength and weakness is that he
has absolutely nothing to do with the acting industry
This is great because this stops me from
Obsessing about my career
Talking about nothing else apart from my career
And putting my head miles up my own arse by
devaluing anything anyone else does for a living that
isn't my career

The downside is Matthew tends to think I'm a cunt
for cancelling on him last minute when an audition
comes up
Ashamed because I don't necessarily advertise us as a
couple to industry folk
When you're my casting, the last thing you want to
be doing is parading around your rainbow arsehole
And most importantly
He doesn't understand why I persist at a career
which only pays me
On average
Three grand a year?
Obviously that doesn't include other work I then do
but Matthew can't seem to grasp the concept that it
isn't about money and that it's a
Lifestyle choice
I guess
And you never know one day
Could get absolute fucking riches
Raining plastic tens
Shitting out coins
I tell him it depresses me that his days are spent on
excel spreadsheets staring at other people's money
But my point is often defeated by the fact these
conversations are over a dinner that he's paid for
Again
In fact his sister
Who is best described as an interfering cunt
Is forever telling Matthew that I'm a gold-digger
And that
Not only am I just using him for financial security
Which I can't lie obviously helps me in what I do

But she claims that I don't even remotely like him
That I am only with him for his money
Which is just an outright lie

He also has a fucking magical dick

Anyway
These are the kind of things Matthew relayed to me
when he decided we go on a break
But we're over that now

MATTHEW: You look
Um
Lovely

It's our anniversary and Matthew's been a basic bitch
and booked us a table at the Aqua Shard
I can tell he's dead excited to take a photo with a
view before putting it on Facebook

We're a bottle and a half of wine down about to order
desert
And Matthew has got progressively more red and
sweaty as the night's gone on

MATTHEW: I've been
Um
I've been meaning to tell you something all night

Okay

MATTHEW: Well
Um
Not so much tell as

Um
Ask?

Oh fuck

MATTHEW: That makes it sound like I'm about to
Sorry
I'm not going to ask you
That
Um
Oh no
Are you upset?

No
Fuck no
That's good
Don't
Don't ask me that please

MATTHEW: Good
I think

Spit it out Matthew Jesus fucking Christ

MATTHEW: Sorry
Yes
Um
I was thinking that
I'm very happy with how things are going
I'm at a point in my life where I want to take the
next steps to
You know
Settling down
With you

I

Um

Love you very much and in my anniversary card
there's a key
To my flat

Well that's a way to ruin a surprise

MATTHEW: I would like you to live with me
I won't charge you rent
Just bills
On the proviso that in the next few years we save
Together
For a place of our own
And this means
Um
I know you love your career and I love that about
you
I'm not saying stop in any form at all

Good

MATTHEW: Yes
But I do think this will give you the opportunity to
be more fiscally responsible
Towards our relationship

Fiscally?

MATTHEW: So
Um
What do you think?
Will you move in with me?

He's staring
Proper intense puppy kind of staring into my eyes
I feel like my soul is being strip searched and he's
going to read every thought that runs through my
deceptively small head
I mean it's too soon it's too

Just bills

Maybe it won't be so bad
I can relax a bit
Sex whenever we want

The thing I love about Matthew is the ability he has
Despite being such a man
To look and behave like a small vulnerable child
When I look at him I just see this geeky little ten
year old who probably used to shit himself
It's really hard to say no

I mean
Yeah
Why not?

It makes sense doesn't it?

Thank you
Thank you

Blows kisses to fans

Thank you

Wow
I can't believe this is really happening
Artist of the year
I just want to take this moment to thank my mum
You're my hero
Thank you for always believing in me
And finally thank you to my fans

Blows more kisses

I love you

VOICE: Okay
So we need much much more energy
You can be crazier
You've just won artist of the year
Use the torch
Remember who you're thanking
Maybe your bosses, the people who have got you
where you are
And most importantly remember what this is for
Punked
We need to hear the product

Phone rings

Phone rings out

MAN: I can see you're online boy

Phone rings again

Phone rings out

    You stood me up

MAN: I'm sorry

    I looked like a fucking idiot

MAN: I was with my colleague, I couldn't get away

    You could have messaged
    I'm not here for weird games
    Either you want to meet up or you don't

MAN: I do lol
    It's tricky. I'm here for work and don't want a
    colleague to see

    This is just a bit
    How do I know you're you?

You won't even tell me your name

MAN: If I tell you will you answer?

No

MAN: Ha
Call me Daniel
Or Sir

Sir Daniel?

MAN: Which one you choose will set the tone of the chat

I'll go with Daniel

MAN: What a pity
Let me take a photo. Show you it's me

You can do three fingers

MAN: Sorry?

To prove it's you
Hold three fingers up to prove it's you

MAN: You never did that for me

You've seen me on stage

MAN: Okay that's blurry

That is

Less blurry
No fingers though

MAN: That depends who's in charge here

Don't you like a challenge?

MAN: No

Ha

MAN: Although you are a deadly combination
Joking aside you're very talented

You keep saying
I would take a picture but I'm not even a passable
five out of ten right now
I'm a solid three

MAN: Wearing?

A football top

MAN: Right

I'll take a photo after I have a shower
But only if I get a three finger picture to prove it's
genuinely you and not a predator
Laughing crying face emoji

You have see-through hands

MAN: Lol bad pad
You can see what I was trying to do
Now
Underwear?

What about them?

MAN: Let me see

MAN: Maybe this isn't for you

What isn't?

MAN: Come on boy
Let me see

MAN: How are you single?

Why is the sky blue?

MAN: Touché
Now lower

MAN: Bit better

Are you the connoisseur of underwear pics?

MAN: Yes
You're gonna be discreet right?

Course
You don't have to worry I'm not about to scream
shit from the rooftops

MAN: I've got a casting call in five minutes

Casting call?

MAN: Yeah

For?

MAN: A film lol
I'm an exec with a lot of power
Does that turn you on?

No
It's a job

MAN: Lol
Liar
I'll call you later

Hello

Hi Rebecca it's Tom

Yes

No not urgent just
Um
Wanted to know if Damien had been in touch?

Castings
If anything's

Right

No I

It's just that it's been a few months and he said that
he'd be calling me in

I understand
Busy
Yes

Alright
Tha-

Hello?

MATTHEW: Why is the sky blue?

Matthew's red again
And this time it's definitely not nerves
I can see veins popping out of the side of his red head
Looks like Voldemort but sunburnt

MATTHEW: You tell me Tommy

Tell you what?

He reaches into his jean pocket
They're tight so it takes an awkwardly long time
He pulls out my phone
And just stands there

Fuck

Before you flip out please let me explain because
there is actually a logical explanation for this

MATTHEW: You went to meet him

For a drink

MATTHEW: I've seen the conversation

So then you would have seen that I never-

MATTHEW: You've sent pictures of yourself
Pictures that you've taken for him in your underwear
Pictures I have never even seen

I don't like him

MATTHEW: I wouldn't expect that you've yet to meet the
man
And I
Um
Understand
I guess
A flirt
But you went to meet him with the intention of
sleeping with him

I didn't

MATTHEW: You did

        I wanted to
        String him along
        Tease him
        It's hard to explain
        But I promise you have nothing to worry about
        It's a weird networking thing

MATTHEW: Networking?
        Tom

        He's in the industry
        I can't just slack him off or he won't work with me

MATTHEW: You did with that casting director last year

        And look where that got me

MATTHEW: Tommy you're actively flirting
        You're sending him photos
        You tell him he's attractive

        He is attractive

MATTHEW: Well this is the thing isn't it
        That's why this is a serious problem
        This is unfaithful

        I needed him to fancy me
        Rope him in and then friend zone him
        I was never going to sleep with him

MATTHEW: That's ludicrous Tom

It's totally

Wreckless

Even if that is true

That is stupidity

That is stupidity at its dictionary definition

I don't expect you to understand

MATTHEW: So what are you going to do?

Are you going to carry on speaking to him?

Because I'm obviously not

Um

Okay with that

I'm not going to do anything

MATTHEW: This is a lot Tom

What you're putting on me

Testing me with

It's a lot

I put up with a lot and make exceptions for what you
want to do

But it's not normal

And even after the exceptions I make for you

You are not acknowledging that you've taken it too
far

You haven't apologised

You haven't taken a look at what you've done

What you've encouraged

And apologised to me for the way that has made me
feel

I'm sorry

MATTHEW: And what's more frightening is the way that
you've demeaned yourself
That is frightening Tommy
Imagine if he'd turned up
God knows the situation you might have got yourself
into

I know what I'm doing

MATTHEW: You don't Tommy
In the grand scheme of things you're a child
You might be intelligent but you are not in control
In a situation like that
By your very standing
With where you are in your career
You would not be in control
It's silliness
You're smarter than that
It's borderline

What?

MATTHEW: No it doesn't matter

What?

MATTHEW: It's borderline prostitution really
It's not healthy for you
And if that is the streak it encourages in you I

suggest you find another path that will make you
just as happy

This isn't working

MATTHEW: What do you
          Um
          What?

          This isn't
          We aren't working

MATTHEW: Let's not get
Um
Carried away now

I'm sorry but we're not
The only reason I moved in with you was because I didn't
have to pay rent
I'm using you
Tell me how that's working?

MATTHEW: That is
That's a nasty thing to say

MATTHEW: I don't want you to do this

I'm sorry
But I do

VOICE: Don't worry
Take your time
Now start again

WOOO
Fuck yeah
Scream for me bitches

I can't hear you!

WOOOOO

Right
Thank you
Thank you

Blows kisses to fans

Thank you

Blows more kisses to fans

Wow
I can't believe this is really happening
PUNKED
That's right
PUNKED artist of the year
I just want to take this moment to thank my mum
Yeah
WOOOO

Blows more kisses to fans

You are my fucking hero
My team
This is for all of you too. I could never have done it
without you
Thank you so much
And finally thank you to my fans

Blows more kisses

I love you

Peace out mother fuckers

WOOOOOOOO

How was that?

DAMIEN: Thank you for coming in

Thank you for seeing me

DAMIEN: It's been a while
Okay so it's just a small part today
But it would be a great first TV credit

Absolutely

DAMIEN: You've read the episode?

I think it's excellent

DAMIEN: Good
It is

DAMIEN: Alright then Tom
In your own time

"Maggie. How are you?"

DAMIEN: *(in audition)* Well

"You look it"

DAMIEN: *(in audition)* Thanks

"I know you are probably getting this all the time
right now and I'm sorry because it must be bringing
it all back every time someone says it but I am

Thinking of you. We all are.
Is there anything we can do to help at all?"

DAMIEN: *(in audition)* No

"Course. Silly question.
You can call anytime. I mean that."

DAMIEN: Alright
That's it

Thank you for seeing me

DAMIEN: You did a great job
That was an excellent take. Well done for being off
book

Of course

DAMIEN: Actually
Before you go

DAMIEN: I did just want to say
About the last time I saw you
I hope you don't think I was being inappropriate

What do you mean?

DAMIEN: At the theatre
The suggestion of a drink

Oh no
Not at all

DAMIEN: Good
I'm glad

DAMIEN: It's just you didn't ask me for coffee

Sorry?

DAMIEN: You said you wanted to grab a coffee instead
The next week
I never heard from you

DAMIEN: I found it incredibly strange that an actor in your
position would snub me
A casting director at the biggest nation television
organisation in the country
A coffee meeting

It was never meant / to be a snub

DAMIEN: Unless of course he thought I was being
inappropriate in asking him if he would like a drink
Which of course certainly wasn't the case

I promise I didn't thought you were being
inappropriate
I'm so sorry that I've been so rude

DAMIEN: No no that's okay
        I just wanted to clear up that little misunderstanding
        Because misunderstandings like that can entirely
        destroy a career which someone has spent decades
        Literally decades building up
        Imagine that
        Over a misunderstanding

        Yeah
        No that's
        That would be crazy

DAMIEN: Yes

DAMIEN: Alright
        Thanks Tom

MAN: I'm going to ask you a question
        I want you to think about it
        And if you answer with a photo of you licking your
        lips
        We'll do it
        How slutty you feeling right now?
        As I'm about to audition three guys from the states

I'm confused
Haha

MAN: I'm tempted to add you to my list
If you'd like that
You know what to do
But you need to be very DL

How do I know you're not some seedy guy lying to get into my bed?

MAN: Lol
You're crazy
Up to you stud

Look I find you very attractive but I'm not the kind of guy to sleep with someone for a part
I sleep with someone because I find them attractive

MAN: Lol
That's not how it works
Plus I'm casting some big names

MAN: Just thought it would be fun to audition you stud
Can tell this isn't for you

If you want to audition me, audition me in my own
right and we can have fun separately
I'm not talking to you for a part. I just think you're
hot
And want to meet with you for fun

MAN: I think you've misunderstood

Clarify for me then

MAN: I'm joking
I'm not serious it's like a fantasy
Power role play

Okay

MAN: Relax
Go along with it
It's fun

It's weird

MAN: After your show
I want to meet you
In costume
I'm going to take you to a hotel
You're going to lap dance for me
Beg me to make me to make you famous
Suck my thick powerful dick
Lick my hard round balls
And then I'm going to basically trash your actor
body

Haha
Good luck getting my costume
Stage manager is an absolute dragon keeper

MAN: Right boy
Should sir watch porn?

No

MAN: So?

I'm in bed
Wink face emoji

MAN: Wearing?

Shorts

MAN: Perfect
Want an order boy?

Go on

MAN: Go on??

Go on
Sir

MAN: Better
Hmmm

I want a full video
Make me cum
You in your shorts
Making a self tape
Cast for me
Beg for the part
Beg to be famous
Tell me what could be mine if I give it to you
I want you to be really vocal
And cum begging to be a star
Talk me through your best assets boy

I'm not really comfortable with that

MAN: It's acting

It's my career
It's a bit close to the bone
I'd rather just meet you
Get to know you

MAN: Lol
Come on
It's fun

People can hear me

MAN: Try boy
Tell me why they're so good

My assets?

MAN: Yeah

I think they speak for themselves sir

MAN: Sell them boy
Can I hear a yes sir?

Can't we just take some pictures sir?
I have to leave for theatre in ten minutes
Nearly six o clock

MAN: No boy
I thought it was almost five there?
Does sir deserve this?
What does sir deserve boy?
Hope you're not going to disappoint

What's the part?

MAN: I thought you wanted roleplay boy?

No you said it was role play

How am I supposed to roleplay an audition if I don't
know what the part is?

MAN: You sexy fuck
What part do you want?

I'd want it to be classy
Something that would go to Cannes

MAN: Really
       See what I was thinking about before was Star Wars
       Seriously
       We need a brit
       And you have the right face
       I can help you

       You're seriously confusing me now

MAN: You're being proud
       I can help you
       Really help you. In real life
       You should see my boys
       I think they would surprise you. They are very high
       profile names
       I help them and they help me
       If you wanted this to be more
       I can help

MAN: Record yourself
       In the way I ordered
       Say yes sir

       Don't have time in the way you ordered

MAN: I'm in charge here you sexy fuck
       Doing this will make you cum quicker
       Am I worth it?

Send me your location
I don't know you. I haven't even met you yet
You could be anyone

MAN: I sent three fingers

Prove you are who you say you are

MAN: I thought you wanted roleplay?

If you don't do it I'm blocking you now

Location sent

MAN: There boy
Now do as I say

MAN: Boy

Phone rings. Tom doesn't answer. He if frantically checking his phone

MAN: Boy is being naughty

MAN: You're scaring me now

Phone rings. Tom rejects

MAN: Fucking answer boy

MAN: Boy

          Sorry
          I'm back

MAN: What were you doing?

          I was checking that you hadn't sent a fake location

MAN: Wow
          Boy is crazy
          What did you find?

          That it's not
          Fake

MAN: Yes
          Boy is naughty
          When I'm back in London I'm going to buy some
          oversized toys for moments like this
          Now stop being a bad little actor bitch
          Time for you to perform

          I'll do it another time

MAN: Fine
          How slutty will the video be?

MAN: I said
How fucking slutty is this self tape gonna be?
How vocal you gonna be?

I need to go

MAN: I'm going to make my boy a star
And in return you'll be my fuck toy

MAN: If you want you can just simply say
This is real sir
At the start of the tape
And you will get an audition
In real life
And I promise you will get the role. No fucking
around here
If you don't say it. Fine
We will just have role play fun with no strings

MAN: But if you say it
If you do that remember
You can't just get what you want and leave
My boys are a long-term thing
Beg sir to be famous

REBECCA: Hi Tom it's Rebecca

Hi Rebecca
How are you?

REBECCA: Yes Tom I'm good I'm good
Look
I've heard from Damien

Yes?

REBECCA: Yes
Hmm
Before I start can I ask is there anything that I
should know about that is happening in your
personal life?

What do you mean?

REBECCA: Death's in the family
Break-ups
Divorce

Why?

REBECCA: Right
This is a bit of an awkward call actually Tom
I spoke to Damien and he said that you weren't off-
book
Not only that but that you hadn't prepared the scene
at all

I'm sorry?
No Rebecca I /

REBECCA: I'm not interested in excuses Tom
Do you know who he is?

Of course I know who he is but I / was

REBECCA: As frustrating as it is, I understand when an actor
has a bad day
That happens
But what I can't and won't abide from anyone on my
books is ill-preparation and
From the sounds of it, simply not caring
I have too many clients who would kill for that
opportunity and you blew it
Do you understand that?

I was off-book

REBECCA: He says you weren't
Why would he lie?

I

REBECCA: Yes?

I don't
Know

REBECCA: This is a real shame

He also told me that he offered you a coffee

And that you didn't even get back to him

This is the casting director that plucked you out of no-where

He told me in no uncertain terms to sign you

I wouldn't have even have been at that show if it wasn't for him

And you can't even go for a coffee with him

It wasn't like that

REBECCA: Enough Tom I don't have time to waste on this phone call

As of next week when you finish your play you won't be on my books anymore

I'll keep you on until then

But after that you're off

REBECCA: And I don't think I have to tell you that you shouldn't come to me for a reference

---

I fucking hate New Years

And this year's going to be especially shit after

It's not like Matthew and I ever actually did anything good

We usually ended up spending it with his family

Which was obviously dry as fuck

But at least I wasn't totally and utterly sad and
alone on the biggest night of forced fun that's ever
existed ever

John has taken up big brotherly duty and duly
invited me to a party with him
When Matthew and I ended I had no choice but to
move back home
Which fucking sucks
There's nothing that could possibly make you feel
more of a failure than moving back to a small town
But anyway it's free rent so I can save and be back in
London in no time
And the commute is only an hour and a half
So it's not actually that bad

CHRIS: Fucking hell. Haven't seen you in a long time
Aren't you supposed to be in Hollywood by now?
Thought you'd be a bit too good for this no?

Here we fucking go

Tom laughs over enthusiastically

CHRIS: You're looking well mate
What brings you here?

I look at John like don't fucking say anything
I've made the decision I'm not gonna tell anyone I've
moved back
Which he said is stupid because everyone will figure
it out anyway but it's not up for discussion

Holidays

CHRIS: John said you got a part in a film

What he's actually referring to is an unpaid short film with the Eastbourne film-makers society

It's nothing really
Just a small part

JOHN: No it's not
You said you're the lead
You know Toms' mate is on Titans

Marcus

CHRIS: Fuckoff
Really?
Which one?

JOHN: Sydney's boyfriend

CHRIS: Your mate is banging Sydney?

Fictionally yes

CHRIS: You should ask him to get you an audition

It doesn't really work like that

CHRIS: No harm in asking
Tell them about your film. I'm sure you'll get one

He gets out his phone

What's he doing?

CHRIS: What's this film called?

Sorry?

CHRIS: What's the film called?

Um
What's Beneath

CHRIS: Is it scary?

Depends how much of a pussy you are

CHRIS: It's not on IMDB
I can't see it on here
Just some film with Michelle Fif. Fiffy-
How do you say that?

Pfeiffer

CHRIS: Who else is in it?
I'll google it

No one

CHRIS: Fucking hell that's a big part then

No it's just
I can't say
You won't find it on google yet. It's secret

CHRIS: Fuckoff
Who am I gonna tell?

Doesn't matter mate
I'm contracted
It's really not big deal

CHRIS: Must be someone famous then

It's really not

CHRIS: Fucking hell put us all to shame why don't ya
I've gotta go back to real work next week

No seriously you know what?
Good on ya son
Nice to see someone from the village done good

Does anyone want a drink?

I did actually try and get them a drink
Mainly to spit in Johns but after a half an hour wait,
when I was finally served my card was rejected
That hurt
So I hibernate in the smoking area for pretty much
the rest of the night
I've tried to make pointless conversation with people
but everyone looks about five
They're talking about what they're going to do when
they leave here
Uni
Jobs
Dreams
I have no idea who the fuck any of these children are

JOHN: Alright

I can tell he's sorry

Alright

JOHN: I'm-

It's fine John
You've got nothing to be sorry for

JOHN: Mum and I are really fucking proud of you you know
You know that

Cringing hell

You're smashed John

JOHN: We are
You might not be where you wanna be but you'll get
there
I know it
And I don't say it enough
You're the hope of the family you know that don't
you?

John

JOHN: I mean it
You are
Both of us think that

You're gonna regret being so nice to me in morning

64

JOHN: Probably

From inside:
10
9
8

JOHN: Fuck
Come on
Quick

5
4
3
2
1

Tom's phone buzz'

MAN: Happy new year boy

Matthew

Matthew

I know you're there
I can literally see you're online

You know you'll give in and say hi in less than five
minutes so can you just save us the time please

I'm sorry
I obviously made a massive mistake

Again

Matthew

Matthew

When you go through school
As in ordinary school
Primary

Secondary

State or private

You are always taught that the harder you work

The bigger the payoff

The more successful you become

Bigger house

Fancier car

Bigger brands draping off of you. Surrounding you fucking

Then you're lucky enough to go to drama school

And of course outside of the physical craft of acting

In terms of trying to search for acting work that premise certainly still applies

But I originally found it such a mind fuck that the harder I worked

On acting

The physical art of acting

The worse I would be

I've always been such a determined cunt and I know what I want for myself

I know what I need my life to be

So I always found

Letting go

And not working hard on my acting but

Working smart

Incredibly difficult.

And then you start your path

Your flight into work and

Years of working hard out of a job

Countless emails

Rejections via never hearing

Blunt rejections from characters so busy they need to

lash out at someone for increasing their workload by
just an extra click of the archive button
Minimum wage
Waiting tables walking dogs answering phones
Then you finally get the job
The acting job
For below minimum wage but it's all worth it
because nothing quite matches that feeling of
Release
The electricity of
Doing it
Fuck it's
It makes me want to just
Cry
Sadness joy everything
Just cry

But all of a sudden it's years and
Obviously expenditure's still higher than income and
there is not a fucking chance
There is not a fucking chance in hell of giving up
I love this too much and I'm so close I can feel it. It's
there. It's waiting. And what is there left?
Honestly
Anything else
I think I'd kill myself
Slit my wrists
Truly
I would
So something's gotta
Something's gotta

MUM: You don't seem yourself at the moment my boy

Can you not call me that?

MUM: What love?

You know what
That

MUM: What
Boy?

Stop it
Just don't call me that

MUM: I always call you that

Well stop it please
I mean it
Alright
I don't like it

MUM: Okay
I'll stop

MUM: Have you heard from Matthew?

No

MUM: I'm sorry to hear that

I'm not

MUM: Is there anyone else?

No
Leave it mum

MUM: Why?

There are things that you just aren't supposed to tell
mums
Rules
Sex, drugs and missed meals
Is generally the rule right?
But with mum it's not because she would be
disapproving it's that
It's just that it's your mum isn't it?

Regardless of that I'm telling her everything

MUM: You haven't gone and got feelings for him?

No
God no
I have absolutely no respect for him he's a cunt

MUM: Good

Obviously I'm not gonna do it mum I just
Needed someone to tell

MUM: Of course
You can tell me anything

MUM: Do you want to do it?

No

MUM: Don't just say that because I'm your mother

I'm not
It's just
It's weird isn't it

MUM: You're so sensitive sweetheart
You're like me
You feel things too much and it leaves you open to
getting hurt
I sometimes wish you weren't but I don't want you
to change
You're my beautiful talented handsome b-

MUM: You know
It wasn't that long ago
You know a lot of female medical students
It was known that they would often have to work
Almost like call girls
Throughout their time as students
To pay for their courses
And then as soon as they became doctors they'd stop
There's absolutely no shame in it

MUM: If you can emotionally handle it
There's no shame in you doing it

You've only got one shot at this life
God knows I wish I had a passion like yours
If it's what you want you should do whatever it takes
to get it my babe
And a lot of people want it so
Just as long as you're safe
Don't put yourself somewhere where you're going to
get hurt

Hello Sir
This is your boy reading for Star Wars
And I'm here to show you what you can have if I get
the role

Fuck

Hello sir

COME ON

Hello sir
This is your rock hard slutty boy reading for Star
Wars

I'm about to show you what you'll get on tap if you
make me a superstar

Oh and by the way
This is real sir

Marcus

I hate seeing people I know when I'm money working
And there is no one
There is no one you would like to see less when
waiting table than Marcus

MARCUS: Oh my gosh Tom
It's been so long
What the devil are you doing here?

Working

MARCUS: You never said
That's cool
Well in that case
Table for two please
My agent's just coming
Shame you can't join us

Shame

MARCUS: So what are you up to?
What's going on?

Just
You know
Plodding along
Auditions and stuff

MARCUS: Oh that's cool

Potentially got something very exciting in the mix
actually

MARCUS: Oh wow
What is it?

Can't really
Sorry I-

MARCUS: Right
I get you
Know that feeling all too well
I'm actually buying Oliver
My agent
Dinner tonight because he's been so good to me
Got me into the final two for something big
Like really big
Like Hollywood big
But because of everything that's going on out there
at the moment it's all a bit up in the air
All rather delayed
Crazy stuff hey?

This is the last thing I want to talk to him about

MARCUS: Very interestingly

You remember Cynthia?

Third year the year before we started

Did that horror film

About the sharks

The remake

MARCUS: Exactly

It happened to her

Producer had her get on her knees for that job

If I don't say anything maybe he'll stop talking

about it

MARCUS: For a horror film as well

That shit got three point two on IMDB

She could have at least done it for something good

Cunt

MARCUS: Still I can't believe how it's all blown up

Bit much if you ask me

MARCUS: Would you?

Sorry?

MARCUS: You're gay

If some guy offered you a job

Big fucking Hollywood film

Would you suck his cock?

Why are you asking me that?

MARCUS: It's fun
Would you?

Fun?

MARCUS: Come on Tom

Would you?

MARCUS: I'm not gay am I?

That doesn't mean you can't suck a cock

MARCUS: Jesus Tom steady on

Would you?

MARCUS: Of course not. I don't reek of desperation
And I don't need to

I fucking hate myself

MARCUS: Anyway this job
I'm like you
Can't say anything about what it is
Sworn to secrecy

Give it a minute or two
He will

MARCUS: Go on tell me

What's the project?

I can't honestly

MARCUS: Oh you old spoil sport

Star wars
It's
The new Star Wars
They're looking for a brit
So
Yeah
Still. Don't wanna get my hopes up just yet but
I think I've got a good chance

MARCUS: Well
I'll be damned
Well done Tom
I
I thought you were just doing theatre but
That's really very good

Thanks

MARCUS: Well I guess it's you or me old pal

Sorry?

MARCUS: Well that's the job
It's you and I in the final two

Oh right
That's
Crazy

MARCUS: What do you think of the script?
Obviously they've churned out loads but holy shit
it's gonna be huge isn't it?

Yeah
It's good yeah
I think it'll be great
Sorry I'm just
This is mental

MARCUS: How did you get in the room for it?
My agent said it was very exclusive

I'm so sorry my manager's just seen me
Let's grab a drink soon though
It's been far too long

MARCUS: Tell him to fuckoff

If only

MARCUS: Well maybe sooner than you think
We really need to hang out more
You should come out and meet the Titans guys
They're great

Sure
I'd really like that

MARCUS: Well good luck
    Jedi buddy
    May the force be with you

Hello sir

Sir it's boy

Need to speak to you
Please

Sir?

My back is weird and flat
There's absolutely no muscle definition
It's just a flat slab of human
Fleshy
Rectangle of boring unsexual flesh
I'm arching it
Doing what I think you are supposed to do to be sexy
My arse is funny

It's just flabby out of nowhere
Out of proportion with the rest of my body
I don't know why I did this position
I actually think this sums me up really well
My life
I'm always doing what I think other people want me
to do
There's a little dildo
Which is really fucking embarrassing
It's pink it's like a joke bullet people buy their
recently single girl friends as a symbol of faux
independence
I put it in my mouth earlier on in the
He had asked me to
When it vibrated it chattered against my teeth
It was like how cartoon characters sound when
they're cold

I've turned around now
I can't look at my face so I'll just focus on my body
and on my

It's small and totally unimpressive
My foreskin's weird it always has been
Probably should have been circumcised
I'm doing this stupid thing where I'm biting my own
lip a lot and I look fucking stupid I want to go back
in time and tell myself to stop doing that I really do
it's fucking shit stop it stop it stop it Tom you stupid
fucking cunt

I fucking hate myself
I look at myself here and I know that he got me

And you look at all these stories in the news
And I feel even more fucking stupid because they
have experienced so much more it's
Fucking actual things
Women
Mainly. Obviously
To them. On their bodies
Harm
And I look at myself here
Grabbing myself
My manhood
You can't see him it's me
Just me
And I hate myself because I only have myself to
I'm the only one I see here
Doing anything. Doing that to myself
And I know what people will think
Especially because of my
Preferences
The gays just like fucking so

For what?
I've done this for what?

MAN: Hi
           Been very busy

Hello sir
I was beginning to think you had gone

MAN: Missed our roleplay a bit
Though with what's been in the news feels far more serious
Reality of it very disturbing. Can't believe some guys

I wondered if the news was why you had been absent

MAN: Ha, no
My boys are a long term thing
Plus, they come onto me. Not the other way around

You free for a call sir?

MAN: Busy

When are you coming over?

MAN: Not sure

What about the casting?

MAN: Self tapes

How's the casting going?

MAN: Well

When's my audition Sir?

MAN: You've had your audition
Winky face emoji

My real one?

I'm friends with Marcus Finchley
I know he's in the final two
I assume I'm the other person?

MAN: He shouldn't be relaying that information

Well he has
Do I not need to audition then?

MAN: You said you wanted roleplay boy

I did
And then I said
This is real sir

MAN: I don't know what you're talking about

MAN: We were just having fun
            I think you've got the wrong idea

            No you said
            You said that was what I was taping for

MAN: I think perhaps we should stop our conversations
            now

            Fuckoff
            No
            I worked for you
            I did what you wanted and I was willing to
            I want your part of the bargain
            I want an audition by Friday

MAN: Lol
            That ain't gonna happen

            Make it happen

MAN: I think you're forgetting who's in charge here

            I haven't deleted our conversations

MAN: So?

            I'll take it to the press
            Seems very topical right now

MAN: And say what?

            Say that you made me do things
            And promised parts

MAN: And who would you say did it?

Daniel
I know where you work

MAN: Lol
Okay

You see the thing is journalists have handy devices
these days
I may not know your name now but I have this
phone number
And they can trace you the fuck down so don't you
laugh at me you power hungry cunt
I will fucking end you
You will see me for an audition
And I will get that part

MAN: I ain't going to listen to some washed up fag fringe
actor
You really think I give desperate guys like you work?
Don't fuck with me boy
I'll end your pitiful career

You have until Friday

MAN: I'm warning you

Friday
Or bye bye all that power
And hello tabloid infamy
You'll become the bitch that drops the soap faster
than you can say boy

MAN: Fuck you

Isn't it funny how on the day something bad happens
I mean really bad
Life changing
Someone dying kind of bad
You remember the tiniest of details about that day
They make such a mark that you can relive the hours
leading up to and after that moment in an absurd
amount of detail
It's like the main thing I remember about the day my
gran died is that I was in the hospital
Downstairs outside the canteen and I was on the
phone to one of my best friends
This is literally five minutes before it happened
And I remember being on the phone in this weird non
corner looking down at the floor
And I can see this floor so vividly
It was a black and white chequered floor
Vinyl tiles
The white slightly faded. Fake grouting around each
square

MATTHEW: Before you ask
I know it's not my job
Um
My place
Anymore

Today I will remember sitting on the floor of my
living room
TV on in the background
The Chase
Bradly Walsh cracking some shit jokes
Sitting there stroking the singular threads on the
inside of my dressing gown five minutes before
Matthew shows up

MATTHEW: I'm not sure exactly what it is you're doing
I didn't want to
Um
Yes

MATTHEW: Your phone's switched off
So I thought that was you
You know
Protecting yourself
Um
I thought you knew

I grab my phone
My shit case always makes it fucking awkward to
turn on so I rip it off
Fucking throw it
God knows where

Phone receives a huge amount of notifications

What the fuck

My phone's glitching from all the messages
Like frozen
Cassie
John
Marcus
Mum

After about two minutes
The longest two minutes you can possibly
My phone
I go on twitter
Hundreds of notifications

Matthew what the fuck is going on?

I click on my dm's
The first one
That'll do
I click it and
There's an article
Someone's sent me I don't even know who I haven't
even registered
Buzzfeed
There's a blurry screenshot I recognise the floor in
the background the shorts the bed

I click on it fast
I can't
My heart is beating like beating fast and hard and it
feels like my head is falling through my chest and
down to my feet and

Video plays:
Fuck
This is for you sir
Make me famous
Please please fucking
Fuck
I'm close
This is for you sir
This

MATTHEW: I told you didn't I?
I did say Tommy
You complete
You fool you absolute
I told you

I run to my room
Slam the door
I can't
This can't be

Phone rings

Phone rings out

Fuck

Phone rings

Hello?
Hello?

I know you can hear me

Take it down
Please
Please. I'm so sorry I threatened you
Please

Please sir
I'm so sorry
Take it down
Please
Please take it down
Take it fucking down
Take it down now

I'm a superstar because I'm super at being a star

VOICE: Okay
Okay Tom very good
Right. Let's take a seat shall we?

I think we need to fess up to something
We aren't actually um
Seeing anyone else for this commercial
We actually
We obviously know who you are and the bosses are
We are well aware of the incredibly large online
following you have and how that all came about
But we think this could be a very good fit
For you, trying to get work
And for us
A new company with big ambitions trying to get
noticed
The humour of it
Of your situation I guess
Will help people connect to us as being a bit
Raw and edgey
Like the line we are launching
So the job is yours on the proviso that you do this
with a bit of tongue in cheek
A knowing glare
Superstar
It's a two year buy-out. Fifty grand a year
And this could be a working partnership for years
and years to come
You just need to embrace it and do the job

VOICE: So if you're interested let's try that again
But how about you give us a little wink at the end of
it this time?
Hey?

END.